NGALI NGA BALUN, NGALI NGA JUGUN

OUR RIVER, OUR COUNTRY

Baryulgil Public School

INDIGENOUS LITERACY FOUNDATION

JINGIIWAALA

We hope you enjoy this special story about our river and our Country. Baryulgil is a rural locality in north-eastern New South Wales, Australia. We are located on the Clarence River in the Clarence Valley Local Government Area. Baryulgil, Malabugilmah and Yulgilbar are situated on the lands of the Bundjalung (Wehlabul) people, who are its Traditional Owners. Our school is small, with an average enrolment of 10 students, each coming from one of the three Communities. Though we are a small school, we have big hearts and work closely with the Community, where our students learn, succeed and thrive, as they grow up on Country at Baryulgil.

–Ashli Ware, Principal of Baryulgil Public School

JINGIIWAALA BLAGANMIRR WITHA BAYAAN

I'd like to begin by telling you my story of the Dirrangun.
This story was told to me when I was a little girl by my grandmother,
Lucy Daley, who was told by her mother and father when she was a little girl.
It is a dreamtime story of how the Clarence River was formed.

Some people say the Dirrangun is a witch,

that she is mean, cunning and brings all the mischief in the world. Others say that she is friendly but a very old woman, who has long hair down to her knees.

Nan said, a long time ago, the Dirrangun lived in Muli Muli. This is where she kept a secret waterhole called Dooloomi. It was the Jurraveel, the home of the Spirit of the water. Dirrangun was greedy and kept it all to herself; she would put leaves and bark all over it to keep it hidden.

But one day, Dirrangun became sick and there was a Balagaan – a strong and beautiful young man.

She asked the Balagaan to go get water from Dooloomi. She had to tell him where it was. So, the Balagaan took a bark coolamon for the water and climbed up into the mountains.

When the Balagaan reached Dooloomi, he saw that Dirrangun had dammed the water up. Enraged by her greed, he broke the dam, letting the water rush out.

It started running and running. Dirrangun came back to the waterhole and saw the water escaping, but she couldn't stop it. She screamed and cried in anger. She chased the water, trying to stop it, but it kept going and going.

It kept going down, creating cascades like rain, filling up creeks and holes, never stopping. The water continued to flow until it rose so high, it carried a fig tree away. The fig tree was washed through the mountains and got caught at Baryulgil, which trapped the water for a while but did not stop it.

THIS IS WHERE MOUNT OGILVIE STANDS TODAY.

Dirrangun, though she tried, could not stop the water, instead she got caught by it and swept away. She was swept over the second pool, which we call Ngalumbeh, where the gorge is today, halfway between here and Copmanhurst.

The water kept going and was unmanageable. Dirrangun continued to try to stop the water. She even sat in the torrent with her legs spread wide apart, strong like tree trunks, trying to keep the water at bay. The water just kept going past her each time, and each time the flood would bury her.

There, where she sat with her legs spread out, with the water rising, is where the south river was made. She sat there until the flood rose higher, sweeping both her and the fig tree on again.

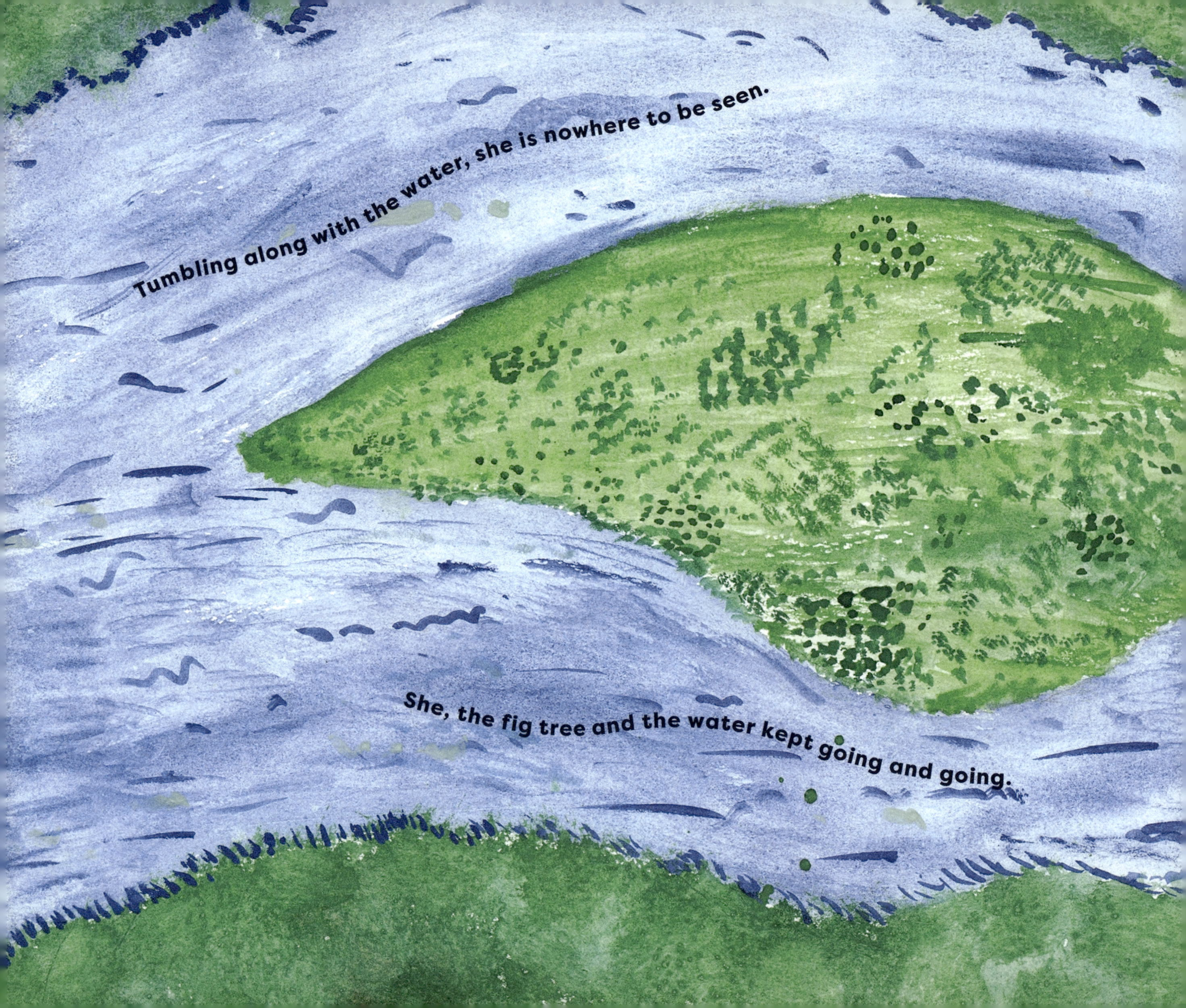

Tumbling along with the water, she is nowhere to be seen.

She, the fig tree and the water kept going and going.

They went all the way down to Maclean.
The fig tree, caught by the land, did not move on from Maclean.
This is where it still stands today.

Dirrangun, however, did not rest. She continued to be swept this way and that by the water, and at last the water came down and went into the sea, which we call in our language burraga.

Yamba is where Dirrangun lies today, you can see her by the lighthouse. Since she could not stop the water, she cursed it with salt and turned herself into stone. This is the big rock down by the lighthouse. This is where she still stands today, the last stand of the Dirrangun.

As the story goes, no one is allowed to remove the rock; if they do there will be a big tidal wave so big that it comes all the way back here to Baryulgil.

Thank you very much

everyone for listening,

or as we say, Bugalbee.

ABOUT THE LONGBRIDGE

The bridge that crosses the Clarence River at Yulgilbar is known to the local people as the longbridge.

It is the place where we swim, go bingiing diving, fishing and relaxing.

We love every bit of the river. We have played there so many times as jarjum running up and down the riverbank, floating downstream, holding on to tree branches and jumping off the bridge.

What a wonderful place to be.

WHAT'S SPECIAL ABOUT THE CLARENCE RIVER?
Jumping off the bridge
The sand and rocks
Diving for turtles
A place to play
The fish, turtles and other animals
Berries and fruit
Many animals live around the river
Making towers with the rocks
Skimming rocks
Sunbake
Food source: bingiing
Jalum: eel-tail catfish, cod, perch, jargan
Meeting place
Quality time with family and friends
Riding down the rapids
Fishing, swimming, kayaking, boating, entertainment
Wrestling in the shallows
BBQ at The Pines
Making sandcastles
Calm
Relax
Splashing
The water gushing over the rocks
The wind rustling through the trees
The sounds
The roar of the water in a flood
The beauty of the water and the Country around it
Small rocks tumbling under the water
Fish jumping out of the water

WHAT'S SPECIAL TO US ABOUT BARYULGIL?

Birds

The wonderful Bundjalung Country

Makes me glad

Guruman, ngamaal, burrubi, buniiny, yambaa, magpie, kookaburra, mibayn, guyaan, jalum

Being around lovely people

Great

The koala on Togetherness Day

Nature

The wonderful students at the school

Sharing stories

Animals moving around

All the beautiful animals

The wind rustling in the trees

Makes me happy

Cows and horses in the paddock

You feel special and wanted and loved

The history of the area

Insects like cicadas screaming

Fish jumping in water

The splashing of the rapids rushing over the rocks

Good to be with your family

Being a part of the community

The sounds of the bush

Adventures and entertainment

Our home

Playing with our pets

Safe

WEHLABUL GLOSSARY

NGALI NGA BALUN, NGALI NGA JUGUN
OUR RIVER, OUR COUNTRY

JINGIIWAALA	HELLO
JINGIIWAALA BLAGANMIRR WITHA BAYAAN	HELLO EVERYONE, HOW ARE YOU TODAY?
DIRRANGUN	WITCH
MULI MULI	SMALL HILLS
DOOLOOMI	TOOLOOM FALLS
BALAGAAN	MAN
BURRAGA	SEA
BUGALBEE	ALL GOOD
JARJUM	CHILDREN
BINGIING	SHORT-NECKED TURTLES
JALUM	FISH
JARGAN	EEL
GURUMAN	KANGAROO
NGAMAAL	GOANNA
BURRUBI	KOALA
BUNIINY	ECHIDNA
YAMBAA	CARPET SNAKE
MIBAYN	EAGLE
GUYAAN	POSSUM

THANK YOU

to the following students who were involved in this project: Dusty, Elhi, Jaali, Jamie, Jewel, Kosszac, Monakiita and Rebel.

Special thanks to Lynette Donnelly for her telling of the River Story, Eloise Walker for her art, Ashli and the Baryulgil PS team for all their hard work day in and day out.

The Bundjalung (Wehlabul) language and traditional story in this book have been shared and edited with the guidance of the Community.

As First Languages are traditionally oral, this text has been transcribed based on Community knowledge.

About the Indigenous Literacy Foundation

The Indigenous Literacy Foundation (ILF) is a national charity working with Aboriginal and Torres Strait Islander remote Communities across Australia. We are Community-led, responding to requests from remote Communities for culturally relevant books, including early learning board books, resources, and programs to support Communities to create and publish their stories in languages of their choice.

In 2024 the ILF won the Astrid Lindgren Memorial Award, given annually to a person or organisation for their outstanding contribution to children's or young adult literature.

First published in 2025 by the Indigenous Literacy Foundation
Gadigal Country
17/207 Kent Street, Sydney NSW 2000
ilf.org.au

Cataloging-in-Publication details are available from the National Library of Australia
www.trove.nla.gov.au

ISBN 9781923179363

Typesetting and design by Holly Doran
Printed in China by RR Donnelley Asia Printing Solutions Limited